Interim Report on 21st Century Cyber-Physical Systems Education

Committee on 21st Century Cyber-Physical Systems Education

Computer Science and Telecommunications Board

Division on Engineering and Physical Sciences

NATIONAL RESEARCH COUNCIL
OF THE NATIONAL ACADEMIES

THE NATIONAL ACADEMIES PRESS
Washington, D.C.
www.nap.edu

THE NATIONAL ACADEMIES PRESS   500 Fifth Street, NW   Washington, DC 20001

NOTICE: The project that is the subject of this report was approved by the Governing Board of the National Research Council, whose members are drawn from the councils of the National Academy of Sciences, the National Academy of Engineering, and the Institute of Medicine. The members of the committee responsible for the report were chosen for their special competences and with regard for appropriate balance.

This project was supported by the National Science Foundation under award number CNS-1341078. Any opinions, findings, conclusions, or recommendations expressed in this publication are those of the author(s) and do not necessarily reflect the view of the organizations or agencies that provided support for this project.

International Standard Book Number-13:   978-0-309-37594-8
International Standard Book Number-10:   0-309-37594-0

Additional copies of this report are available from:

The National Academies Press
500 Fifth Street, NW, Keck 360
Washington, DC 20001
(800) 624-6242
(202) 334-3313
http://www.nap.edu

Copyright 2015 by the National Academy of Sciences. All rights reserved.

Printed in the United States of America

THE NATIONAL ACADEMIES
Advisers to the Nation on Science, Engineering, and Medicine

The **National Academy of Sciences** is a private, nonprofit, self-perpetuating society of distinguished scholars engaged in scientific and engineering research, dedicated to the furtherance of science and technology and to their use for the general welfare. Upon the authority of the charter granted to it by the Congress in 1863, the Academy has a mandate that requires it to advise the federal government on scientific and technical matters. Dr. Ralph J. Cicerone is president of the National Academy of Sciences.

The **National Academy of Engineering** was established in 1964, under the charter of the National Academy of Sciences, as a parallel organization of outstanding engineers. It is autonomous in its administration and in the selection of its members, sharing with the National Academy of Sciences the responsibility for advising the federal government. The National Academy of Engineering also sponsors engineering programs aimed at meeting national needs, encourages education and research, and recognizes the superior achievements of engineers. Dr. C. D. Mote, Jr., is president of the National Academy of Engineering.

The **Institute of Medicine** was established in 1970 by the National Academy of Sciences to secure the services of eminent members of appropriate professions in the examination of policy matters pertaining to the health of the public. The Institute acts under the responsibility given to the National Academy of Sciences by its congressional charter to be an adviser to the federal government and, upon its own initiative, to identify issues of medical care, research, and education. Dr. Victor J. Dzau is president of the Institute of Medicine.

The **National Research Council** was organized by the National Academy of Sciences in 1916 to associate the broad community of science and technology with the Academy's purposes of furthering knowledge and advising the federal government. Functioning in accordance with general policies determined by the Academy, the Council has become the principal operating agency of both the National Academy of Sciences and the National Academy of Engineering in providing services to the government, the public, and the scientific and engineering communities. The Council is administered jointly by both Academies and the Institute of Medicine. Dr. Ralph J. Cicerone and Dr. C. D. Mote, Jr., are chair and vice chair, respectively, of the National Research Council.

www.national-academies.org

OTHER RECENT REPORTS OF THE COMPUTER SCIENCE AND TELECOMMUNICATIONS BOARD

A Review of the Next Generation Air Transportation System: Implications and Importance of System Architecture (2015)
Bulk Collection of Signals Intelligence: Technical Options at the Nexus of Cybersecurity and Public Policy: Some Basic Concepts and Issues (2015)
Emerging and Readily Available Technologies and National Security: A Framework for Addressing Ethical, Legal, and Societal Issues (2014)
Geotargeted Alerts and Warnings: Report of a Workshop on Current Knowledge and Research Gaps (2013)
Professionalizing the Nation's Cybersecurity Workforce? Criteria for Future Decision-Making (2013)
Public Response to Alerts and Warnings Using Social Media: Summary of a Workshop on Current Knowledge and Research Gaps (2013)
Continuing Innovation in Information Technology (2012)
Computing Research for Sustainability (2012)
The Safety Challenge and Promise of Automotive Electronics: Insights from Unintended Acceleration (2012, with the Board on Energy and Environmental Systems and the Transportation Research Board)
Strategies and Priorities for Information Technology at the Centers for Medicare and Medicaid Services (2011)
The Future of Computing Performance: Game Over or Next Level? (2011)
Wireless Technology Prospects and Policy Options (2011)
Public Response to Alerts and Warnings on Mobile Devices: Summary of a Workshop on Current Knowledge and Research Gaps (2011)

Limited copies of CSTB reports are available free of charge from:
Computer Science and Telecommunications Board
National Research Council
The Keck Center of the National Academies
500 Fifth Street, NW, Washington, DC 20001
(202) 334-2605/cstb@nas.edu
www.cstb.org

COMMITTEE ON 21ST CENTURY CYBER-PHYSICAL SYSTEMS EDUCATION

JOHN A. (JACK) STANKOVIC, University of Virginia, *Co-Chair*
JAMES (JIM) STURGES, Lockheed Martin Corporation (retired), *Co-Chair*
ALEXANDRE BAYEN, University of California, Berkeley
CHARLES R. FARRAR, Los Alamos National Laboratory
MARYE ANNE FOX, University of California, San Diego
SANTIAGO GRIJALVA, Georgia Institute of Technology
HIMANSHU KHURANA, Honeywell International, Inc.
PANGANAMALA R. (PR) KUMAR, Texas A&M University, College Station
INSUP LEE, University of Pennsylvania
WILLIAM MILAM, Ford Motor Company
SANJOY K. MITTER, Massachusetts Institute of Technology
JOSÉ M.F. MOURA, Carnegie Mellon University
GEORGE J. PAPPAS, University of Pennsylvania
PAULO TABUADA, University of California, Los Angeles
MANUELA M. VELOSO, Carnegie Mellon University

Staff

VIRGINIA BACON TALATI, Program Officer, *Study Director*
SHENAE BRADLEY, Senior Program Assistant
JON EISENBERG, Director, Computer Science and Telecommunications Board

COMPUTER SCIENCE AND TELECOMMUNICATIONS BOARD

ROBERT F. SPROULL, University of Massachusetts, Amherst, *Chair*
LUIZ ANDRE BARROSO, Google, Inc.
STEVEN M. BELLOVIN, Columbia University
ROBERT F. BRAMMER, Brammer Technology, LLC
EDWARD FRANK, Apple, Inc.
SEYMOUR E. GOODMAN, Georgia Institute of Technology
LAURA HAAS, IBM Corporation
MARK HOROWITZ, Stanford University
FARNAM JAHANIAN, Carnegie Mellon University
MICHAEL KEARNS, University of Pennsylvania
ROBERT KRAUT, Carnegie Mellon University
SUSAN LANDAU, Google, Inc.
PETER LEE, Microsoft Corporation
DAVID E. LIDDLE, US Venture Partners
BARBARA LISKOV, Massachusetts Institute of Technology
FRED B. SCHNEIDER, Cornell University
JOHN STANKOVIC, University of Virginia
JOHN A. SWAINSON, Dell, Inc.
ERNEST J. WILSON, University of Southern California
KATHERINE YELICK, University of California, Berkeley

Staff

JON EISENBERG, Director
LYNETTE I. MILLETT, Associate Director
VIRGINIA BACON TALATI, Program Officer
SHENAE BRADLEY, Senior Program Assistant
EMILY GRUMBLING, Program Officer
RENEE HAWKINS, Financial and Administrative Manager

For more information on CSTB, see its website at http://www.cstb.org; write to CSTB, National Research Council, 500 Fifth Street, NW, Washington, DC 20001; call (202) 334-2605; or email CSTB at cstb@nas.edu.

Preface

Cyber-physical systems (CPS) are increasingly relied on to provide functionality and value to products, systems, and infrastructure in sectors including transportation (aviation, automotive, rail, and marine), health care, manufacturing, and electrical power generation and distribution. CPS are smart, networked systems with embedded sensors, computer processors, and actuators that sense and interact with the physical world (including people); support real-time, guaranteed performance; and are often found in critical applications. Cyber-physical systems have the potential to provide much richer functionality, including efficiency, flexibility, autonomy, and reliability, than systems that are loosely coupled, discrete, or manually operated, but also can create vulnerability related to security and reliability. Advances in CPS could yield systems that can communicate and respond faster than humans (e.g., autonomous collision avoidance for automobiles) or more precisely (e.g., robotic surgery); enable better control and coordination of large-scale systems, such as the electrical grid or traffic controls; improve the efficiency of systems (e.g., "smart buildings"); and enable advances in many areas of science. As CPS become more pervasive, so too will demand for a workforce with the capacity and capability to design, develop, and maintain them.

Building on its research program in CPS, the National Science Foundation (NSF) has begun to explore requirements for education and training. As part of that exploration, NSF asked the National Research Council (NRC) of the National Academies to study the topic and prepare interim and final reports examining the need for and content of a cyber-physical

> **BOX P.1 Statement of Task**
>
> An ad hoc committee will conduct a study on the current and future needs in education for cyber-physical systems (CPS). Two workshops would be convened early on to gather input and foster dialogue, and a brief interim report would be prepared to highlight emerging themes and summarize related discussions from the workshops. The committee's final report would articulate a vision for a 21st century CPS-capable U.S. workforce. It would explore the corresponding educational requirements, examine efforts already under way, and propose strategies and programs to develop faculty and teachers, materials, and curricula. It would consider core, cross-domain, and domain-specific knowledge. It would consider the multiple disciplines that are relevant to CPS and how to foster multi-disciplinary study and work. In conducting the study, the committee would focus on undergraduate education and also consider implications for graduate education, workforce training and certification, community colleges, the K-12 pipeline, and informal education. It would emphasize the skills needed for the CPS scientific, engineering, and technical workforce but would also consider broader needs for CPS "fluency."

systems education. The committee's statement of task is provided in Box P.1. The results of this study are intended to inform those who might support efforts to develop curricula and materials (such as NSF), faculty and university administrators, industries with needs for CPS workers, and current and potential students about intellectual foundations, opportunities, and curricular needs.

To gather perspectives on these topics, the Committee on 21st Century Cyber-Physical Systems Education, appointed by the NRC, convened two workshops (on April 30, 2014, and October 2-3, 2014, in Washington, D.C.) and received briefings from additional experts from the Jet Propulsion Laboratory on June 26, 2014, via teleconference. Chapter 1 summarizes material presented at the workshops and in the briefings. The committee has also conducted initial deliberations and identified several emerging themes, which are discussed in Chapter 2. Following issuance of this interim report, the committee will continue its information gathering and deliberations and issue its final report providing its findings and recommendations later in 2015.

Jack Stankovic and Jim Sturges, *Co-Chairs*
Committee on 21st Century Cyber-Physical Systems Education

Acknowledgment of Reviewers

This report has been reviewed in draft form by individuals chosen for their diverse perspectives and technical expertise, in accordance with procedures approved by the National Research Council's Report Review Committee. The purpose of this independent review is to provide candid and critical comments that will assist the institution in making its published report as sound as possible and to ensure that the report meets institutional standards for objectivity, evidence, and responsiveness to the study charge. The review comments and draft manuscript remain confidential to protect the integrity of the deliberative process. We wish to thank the following individuals for their review of this report:

Ella Atkins, University of Michigan,
Bernd Girod, Stanford University,
Scott A. Hareland, Medtronic, Inc.,
Chenyang Lu, Washington University in St. Louis,
Douglas A. Stuart, Boeing Company,
Janos Sztipanovits, Vanderbilt University,
Daniel Weihs, Technion – Israel Institute of Technology,
Yannis Yortsos, University of Southern California, and
Feng Zhao, Microsoft Research Asia, Microsoft Corporation.

Although the reviewers listed above have provided many constructive comments and suggestions, they were not asked to endorse the conclusions or recommendations, nor did they see the final draft of the report before its release. The review of this report was overseen by Venkatesh Narayanamurti, Harvard University. Appointed by the National Research Council, he was responsible for making certain that an independent examination of this report was carried out in accordance with institutional procedures and that all review comments were carefully considered. Responsibility for the final content of this report rests entirely with the authoring committee and the institution.

Contents

1   SUMMARY OF PRESENTATIONS AND WORKSHOP   1
       DISCUSSIONS
       Industry Cyber-Physical Systems Needs, 1
       Gaps in Skills and Knowledge, 3
       The Evolution of Engineering Education, 5
       Creating CPS-Focused Courses and Programs, 6
           Creating an Introductory CPS Course, 6
           A Proposed CPS Engineering Curriculum, 8
           Building on the Experience of Creating a Computer
               Engineering Program to Create a CPS Program, 8
       Incorporating CPS into Engineering Fields, 8
           Aerospace Engineering, 10
           Civil and Environmental Engineering, 11
       Challenges in Building a CPS Curriculum, 12
       Making CPS More Attractive to Students, 13
       CPS Education Opportunities Beyond the Undergraduate
             Classroom, 13
           Industry-Academic Partnerships, 13
           Internships, 14
           Massive Open Online Courses, 15
           K-12 Education, 16

2   PRELIMINARY OBSERVATIONS   18

APPENDIXES

A	Biographies of Committee Members and Staff	25
B	Presentations to the Committee	35

1

Summary of Presentations and Workshop Discussions

The committee held two workshops in 2014—on April 30 and October 2-3 in Washington, D.C.—to explore the knowledge and skills required for cyber-physical systems (CPS) work, education, and training requirements and possible approaches to retooling engineering and computer science programs and curricula to meet these needs. This chapter provides a brief summary of material presented and discussed at the workshops and during a June 26, 2014, briefing with the Jet Propulsion Laboratory (JPL) via teleconference, organized around themes chosen by the committee.

INDUSTRY CYBER-PHYSICAL SYSTEMS NEEDS

Several speakers from industry spoke about the expected demand for CPS talent. Asked how many individuals with CPS engineering knowledge Ford Motor Company needed, Craig Stephens, with Ford Research and Advanced Engineering, responded "[the] short answer is more than we can get." Joseph Salvo, director at GE Global Research, observed that "going forward . . . almost all of our employees are going to be touched by this."

Describing why demand for CPS talent is growing in the automotive industry, Stephens noted that while basic automobile engineering knowledge (power train, combustion, emissions, etc.) remains fundamental, automotive engineers must also be able to design, develop, and test systems that include communication and sensing technologies and more sophisticated computer controls. These new skills are especially important in new applications such as electrification, vehicle-to-vehicle communication, active safety features, and automated or autonomous driving. Stephens noted that industry has been successful in providing the necessary training, but, looking ahead, companies like Ford hope that employees will enter with a stronger foundation in CPS. Dan Johnson, Honeywell International, Inc., cited aeronautics and aerospace as another transportation industry in which CPS play an increasingly important role. For example, numerous CPS-intensive systems—aircraft, airports, air traffic control, maintenance, passenger services, etc.—make up the air transportation environment.

Jon Williams, a system architect at John Deere, observed that the agricultural and construction equipment sector is increasingly CPS-intensive as well. For example, Deere manufactures partially and fully autonomous vehicles, provides mesh wireless and telematics links between vehicles, updates and repairs its products remotely, and is developing applications for the agronomic data that its products collect. Moreover, Williams noted, a large industrial farm today is a system of systems and requires a systems approach to developing and deploying products and services rather than the traditional focus on individual products.

John Mills, from SimuQuest, Inc., a software company that develops products that support model-based systems engineering, identified key knowledge areas that he is looking for in employees: plant modeling, algorithm design, control system design, network understanding, and engineering process. There is also a new emphasis on CPS skills, including determinism, managing timing and latency, and co-simulation. Mills noted that while Ford, GE, and Deere may have the resources to train their employees in CPS skills, a smaller company like SimuQuest has a harder time doing so.

Scott Hareland, from the medical devices firm Medtronic, Inc., discussed the increasing capability of medical devices to monitor and diagnose health conditions, be life-sustaining (pacemakers), or simply improve life through pain reduction. He noted that while today's engineers are equipped with some of the skills needed to develop future medical devices, there are still several skills they lack.

Clas Jacobson, United Technologies Corporation, contrasted CPS and systems engineering. He noted that systems engineering is centered around four elements: requirements, architecture, model-based development, and design flows. CPS skills complement those of systems engineers, who are able to quickly build models but are unable to analyze and verify them at a system level. Individuals with CPS engineering knowledge are needed to improve quality as functionality is added to systems.

David Nichols and Daniel Dvorak, JPL, briefed the committee on the

CPS needs of JPL, which designs, builds, deploys, and operates spacecraft systems such as the Mars Science Laboratory, the Curiosity rover, and the Cassini orbiter. Jobs at JPL that require CPS skills include mission formulation dealing with autonomy requirements; engineering design at the assembly, subsystem, and system levels; design activities specifically related to autonomous control (fault management, verification and validation, and mission operations); systems engineering at all levels; and mission, software, and safety assurance. JPL tends to develop flight project engineers internally because JPL finds it hard to identify graduates who already possess all the needed CPS and other engineering skills. Indeed, about four-fifths of JPL's science and engineering new hires are recent graduates that JPL intends to develop through hands-on project work and mentoring from senior engineers.

GAPS IN SKILLS AND KNOWLEDGE

Several of the speakers from industry noted that engineers who deeply understand and can apply systems thinking—that is, a deep understanding of how individual parts of a system interrelate with one another and within the system as a whole—and related concepts such as abstraction and system interaction and who can carry out systems analysis using formal methods and model-based verification are in short supply. Nichols and Dvorak from JPL observed that few universities seemed to be emphasizing mission- or safety-critical systems and that hands-on project work tends to ignore properties like fault tolerance and robustness. Stephens from Ford Motor Company also noted that there is a focus on developing new functions over understanding the tools and techniques needed to test and maintain current systems. Mills pointed out that SimuQuest seeks to hire "super engineers," individuals with knowledge in computer science and object-oriented programming; embedded software engineering; experience with hardware, firmware, drivers, BIOS, and controls systems; and plant modeling. Finding individuals with such a wide breadth of skills may seem impractical but is integral in developing new technologies.

Johnson from Honeywell underscored the importance of cybersecurity for engineers in fields like aerospace engineering, where knowledge is needed in such areas as risk management and product integrity, cryptography, and the security of network and communications protocols as well as behavioral and social aspects of security. Williams added that it was important to understand security at the system as well as component level.

Several speakers pointed to challenges working across disciplines. Hareland noted that students need to learn how to work in the cross-functional teams that are needed to build CPS, something that requires both broad knowledge of multiple areas of expertise and excellent communication skills. Unfortunately, Hareland observed, there are countervailing trends toward very deep, narrow, and isolated work, perhaps amplified by the "publish or perish" academic culture, which often serves as a disincentive to interdisciplinary work.

Other "soft skills" were identified as important to creating well-rounded CPS engineers. Nichols and Dvorak noted, for example, that engineers sometimes fail because they simply cannot "read a room" to understand what information at what level is needed by a customer. Additionally, Williams observed that soft skills are especially important when designing for a global market. For example, the diverse regulatory, legal, and standards requirements found around the globe have significant implications for the design process. Solid technical writing and other communications skills are also essential.

Academic presenters identified what they saw as gaps in CPS education today. Sanjai Rayadurgam, Software Engineering Center, University of Minnesota, observed that although traditional undergraduate curricula cover the fundamentals of math and science, programming, and problem solving well, they do less well with applications, software engineering, and problem identification. Students are able to analyze the correctness of components but less equipped to address integration, composition, and other system-level concerns. Rayadurgam noted that students not only need to be able to verify the correctness but convince others of this correctness. Alberto Sangiovanna-Vincentelli, Department of Electrical Engineering and Computer Science, University of California, Berkeley, commented that it was far more important for students to learn design science principles than to master a particular design technique or tool suite. Janos Sztipanovits, Departments of Electrical Engineering and Computer Engineering, Vanderbilt University, discussed the need for a cross-disciplinary view of design. Sztipanovits observed that the traditional way to design starts with functional decomposition to identify major components. These components are then designed, often with a discipline-centric focus; the components are integrated; and the resulting system is subjected to testing and verification. This process often fails because interdependencies are not properly accounted for.

Douglas Adams, Department of Civil and Environmental Engineering, Vanderbilt University, suggested that project-based learning should be integral to any CPS curriculum. Students need to work on complex interdisciplinary projects that encourage systems-level thinking. Doing so requires test beds that allow for the codesign of physical and computational components that demonstrate the benefits of integrating simulation and experimentation. Sztipanovits observed that design studios, where students can work on integrative CPS projects with multidisciplinary teams, are important.

Further discussion by workshop participants identified other skills and knowledge areas needed by a person working in CPS. These include behavior modeling, control systems, uncertainty, information management, embedded systems, embedded system design, and experience working with hardware and firmware.

THE EVOLUTION OF ENGINEERING EDUCATION

CPS are only one of several current drivers of change in engineering education. Norman Fortenberry, American Society for Engineering Education, described some of the attributes expected of modern engineers: flexibility to manage rapidly evolving technologies; an ability to define as well as solve problems; skill and experience with creativity, entrepreneurship, and public policy implications; and facility with both theory and application.

Several speakers noted that engineering students increasingly seek hands-on experience early in their student careers, want to engage in meaningful work with real-world impact, and wish to be entrepreneurial. Furthermore, students tend to be motivated by societally important "grand challenges." For example, students find large-scale projects that address real-world problems in areas like urban sustainability appealing.

Shankar Sastry, University of California, Berkeley, discussed how his institution has responded to such interests. In 2005, Berkeley started the Center for Entrepreneurship and Technology to support the prototyping of projects and a connection to businesses. The Blum Center for Developing Economies, launched in 2007, provides global field study opportunities and other international experiences. The Fung Institute for Engineering in 2010 began offering entrepreneurship opportunities via its Global Venture Lab. The Jacobs Institute for Design Innovation provides hands-on, design, and "maker" experiential learning opportunities for students and working studios for design, iteration, optimization, and commercialization.

Traditionally, students have spent the early part of their undergraduate years fulfilling basic course requirements, whereas students today, some of whom may have been building things in high school, want to continue building new things. Kevin Massey from the Defense Advanced Research Projects Agency, cautioned that students risk jumping too far ahead, not appreciating that an ability to work with plug-and-play hardware and software is not, ultimately, a substitute for foundational knowledge. Massey asked whether it is possible to develop a curriculum that blends both aspects in a way that is both immediately appealing to students and provides them the solid educational foundation they need to be successful in their careers.

CREATING CPS-FOCUSED COURSES AND PROGRAMS

Several presentations provided examples of creating a CPS course or building CPS curricula or programs.

Creating an Introductory CPS Course

Edward Lee, Department of Electrical Engineering and Computer Science, University of California, Berkeley, discussed his experiences teaching a course titled "Introduction to Embedded Systems" with the goal of introducing students to the design and analysis of computational systems that interact with physical processes. Lee also noted that the traditional view of embedded systems assumes special-purpose hardware and that the chief problem is the interface between sensors and actuators and the system's resource constraints. CPS is different—and more interesting—because of the interactions with the physical world.

The principal focus of the course was the interplay of practical design with formal models of systems, including both software components and physical dynamics, with a major emphasis on building high-confidence systems with real-time and concurrent behaviors. Traditional embedded systems classes tend to focus on building the core technical competencies to build systems. By contrast, Lee's course also emphasized critical thinking about systems. What are the pitfalls? Where can improvements be made? Figure 1.1 compares elements of a traditional embedded systems course and a CPS-focused course.

As part of preparing for the course, Lee and coauthor Sanjit Seshia wrote a textbook titled *Introduction to Embedded Systems: A Cyber-Physical Systems Approach*.[1] The text incorporates three distinct threads: modeling (the process of gaining deeper understanding of a system through imitation), design (the structured creation of artifacts), and analysis (the process of gaining understanding through system dissection). Material from a classical embedded systems course makes up much of the design category. The modeling side is focused on cyber-physical system modeling. Topics include modeling the physical using ordinary differential equations, combining discrete dynamics with continuous dynamics, simulation using actor models, and modeling concurrency. The analysis thread provides an introduction to formal methods. Any one of these threads

---

[1] Edward A. Lee and Sanjit A. Seshia, *Introduction to Embedded Systems: A Cyber-Physical Systems Approach*, Edition 1.5, published by authors, 2014, http://leeseshia.org/.

Traditional Focus	Cyber-Physical Systems Focus
Hardware interfacing	Modeling
Interrupts	Timing
Memory systems	Dynamics
C programming	Imperative logic
Assembly language	Concurrency
FPGA design	Networking
Real-time operating system design	Verification

FIGURE 1.1 Elements of traditional embedded systems and CPS-focused courses. NOTE: FPGA, field-programmable gate array. SOURCE: Edward A. Lee, University of California, Berkeley.

could be the subject of a course on its own; in any introductory course, the goal is to introduce these elements and explore their interplay.

Introduction to Embedded Systems supports the threads being read concurrently and also fits nicely within a 15-week semester. Included with the text is a free laboratory manual, which was developed with support from National Instruments. Laboratory projects over the first 6 weeks cover sensors, operating-system-less programming, direct-memory mapping to interact with input/output devices, C language programming, and model-based design, culminating in a robotics challenge. A 9-week capstone project, defined by the students, follows these laboratories. Lee noted that the laboratory portions of any course can became unwieldy to manage, especially as class size grows.

Lee concluded his remarks by expressing hope that by emphasizing modeling, design, and analysis, his course could help students avoid the sort of bruteforce and over-engineering all too often used to build embedded systems today. Also, if students are to be positioned to build the systems of tomorrow, they need to understand not just today's best practices but the weaknesses in those approaches. Lee explained, "Our view is that the field of cyber-physical systems is very young, and it would not serve our students well to leave them with the illusion that completing the course is equated to mastery of the subject."

A Proposed CPS Engineering Curriculum

Tarek Abdelzaher, Department of Computer Science, University of Illinois, Urbana-Champaign, presented a conceptual CPS curriculum. Comparing a more traditional embedded systems course with a CPS-course, Abdelzaher noted that a CPS course must teach students to reason about a system (not just components) that combines interacting computational and physical components and address reliability, robustness, timeliness, performance, and stability requirements. These skills map to fundamental background knowledge in areas such as probability, control, and queuing theory and real-time systems, dynamic systems, and operating systems. Furthermore, students must be able to understand architectural trade-offs and analysis techniques and gain experience designing and implementing CPS given high-level specifications. Abdelzaher's proposed curriculum, including these elements and drawing on existing electrical engineering and computer science curricula, is shown in Figure 1.2.

Building on the Experience of Creating a Computer Engineering Program to Create a CPS Program

André DeHon, University of Pennsylvania, described how Penn's experience developing a computer engineering (CE) program might inform the development of a CPS program. At Penn, the CE program is separate from the electrical engineering (EE) and computer and information science (CIS) departments. It emphasizes embedded systems but is not exclusively CPS. The course requirements for CE include several courses offered by the EE and CIS departments together with a few new CE courses (see Figure 1.3). Several of the courses are not required for either the EE or CIS undergraduate degree but are requirements for the CE degree. As a result, although much of the coursework overlaps with that of other departments, the required coursework is quite different from that in either EE or CIS.

DeHon concluded by considering what would need to be added to the CE program to create a CPS-focused curriculum. He suggested that additional courses would be needed in linear algebra, control, design, and mechatronics or robotics.

INCORPORATING CPS INTO ENGINEERING FIELDS

The committee is interested not only in how one might go about establishing a CPS-focused curriculum or program, but also in how CPS knowledge currently is and might be incorporated into existing engineering programs.

		Advanced Cyber-Physical Systems and Applications			Application Area Electives Dynamic Systems	
Advanced electives, 8th semester, graduate	Formal Methods				Advanced Control	
6th – 7th Semester		Cyber-Physical Systems		Queuing Theory	Feedback Control	
5th – 6th Semester		Embedded Systems (Basic Concepts)		Probability Theory	Dynamic Systems	
3rd – 4th Semester		Systems Programming (Entry-Level OS)	Basic Computer Architecture			

FIGURE 1.2 A model for CPS curriculum. Courses highlighted in gray focus specifically on CPS, while the other courses are existing courses. SOURCE: Tarek Abdelzaher, University of Illinois, Urbana-Champaign.

Courses from
Computer and Information Science
- Programming
- Discrete math
- Data structures/algorithms
- Computer organization
- Computer architecture
- Operating systems

Courses from
Electrical Engineering
- Electronics (RLC circuits)
- Digital design
- Embedded systems
- Networking

New Computer Engineering Courses
- Life-critical embedded systems
- Circuit design for digital engineering
- Digital audio

Courses to Add for a Cyber-Physical Systems Program
- Linear algebra
- Control
- Design
- Mechatronics or robotics

FIGURE 1.3 Coursework for computer engineering (and cyber-physical systems). NOTE: RLC, resistance (R), inductance (L), and capacitance (C). SOURCE: André DeHon, University of Pennsylvania.

Aerospace Engineering

Jonathan How, Massachusetts Institute of Technology (MIT), discussed the need for CPS skills in aerospace engineering. He started by describing emerging applications of aerospace engineering, such as supporting wired and wireless network communications, expanding use of unmanned vehicles, commercial access to low Earth orbit, and addressing environmental and energy challenges as air travel continues to grow. How noted that MIT's AeroAstro department has been working to identify the long-term competencies associated with these applications and build up its faculty in those areas, many of which overlap with CPS knowledge and skills. Key areas include design of aerospace vehicles; real-time aerospace information science; advanced computation methods to support design and decision-making; human-system collaboration; atmospheric science and how it informs system design; and the design, implementation, and operation of complex aerospace systems.

Cutting across these core competencies, there is a broad focus on systems. Students learn to appreciate the challenges of larger-scale "missions" and the cost, complexity, and time that must be invested in both hardware and software aspects of a system. Other cross-cutting themes include software, which has become ubiquitous in aerospace systems, and communications networks and security.

Coursework places a significant emphasis on experimental and systems design, allowing students to develop technical depth through hands-on activities.

How listed the following areas where CPS curriculum could improve:

- Give students design problems with larger scope and cross-disciplinary mission goals, including problems that involve multiple departments and run across multiple semesters.
- Emphasize development of communications skills.
- Evolve the core control curriculum, which has been static for many years, to better reflect CPS fundamentals and applications.
- Increase the emphasis on software and computing in the design process for systems taught to students.
- Address technologies for use of multiple sensors.
- Place greater emphasis on human-systems interaction and human factors design issues.

How concluded by underscoring that it was important not only to impart particular knowledge and develop particular skills, but also to create lifelong learners who can adapt to new technologies, tools, and problems.

Civil and Environmental Engineering

Jerry Lynch, University of Michigan, discussed how CPS technologies have had significant impact on civil and environmental engineering (CEE) in applications such as intelligent transportation systems, earthquake early-warning systems, flood control, and real-time monitoring of smart buildings. CPS-rich intelligent infrastructure is an emerging and important subdiscipline of CEE. CPS technologies make it possible to detect and collect large sets of data from structures and create new opportunities to monitor and study them. CPS technologies are attracting students both because they make CEE appear more "high tech" and because they help make possible advances in two compelling applications of CEE—urban sustainability and community resiliency. In response to new technology opportunities and changing student interests, the University of Michigan has hired CPS-oriented faculty and created a new graduate program in intelligent infrastructure. Much of the faculty who participate have dual degrees in CEE and electrical and computer engineering.

Lucio Soibelman, University of Southern California, discussed the graduate program his school has created in advanced infrastructure systems. He noted that a particular challenge is teaching the necessary graduate-level computer science material to civil engineering graduates, who often lack a strong foundation in computer science.

Christopher Gill, Washington University in St. Louis, used a current research project on structure modeling to demonstrate the importance of interdisciplinary CPS research teams. One of the project's experiments used the response to stress of a piece of a structure in a simulation of the full structure. Such work requires knowledge and skills from computer science, computer engineering, mechanical engineering, and civil engineering. Gill also noted a conflict between what can be done and what needs to be done. Data can be provided very quickly—a millisecond interval for refreshing and delivering actuation commands—but do civil engineers need that much data? Does the physical phenomenon have such a high dynamic? Can the model provide additional detail over faster data during the time interval? In conclusion, Gill reiterated that separate disciplines have much to teach each other, and research topics that interlock with other disciplines help students develop both depth and breadth.

CHALLENGES IN BUILDING A CPS CURRICULUM

Several speakers addressed the related questions of how the teaching and research capacity needed to support CPS education can be built and what other resources are needed to support CPS education.

In his remarks, Christopher Gill observed that the situation with CPS today resembles the one roughly two decades ago with distributed real-time embedded systems, when knowledge and skills from the distinct areas of real-time systems, software engineering, and distributed systems had to be integrated. Support from varying organizations and agencies helped to build communities across previous boundaries, and today, with CPS knowledge spread across multiple research disciplines and educational programs, a similar integration effort is needed. Gill noted that agency coordination and investment is needed.

Jerry Lynch observed that the next generation of faculty in many areas of engineering and computer science will need a broad exposure to CPS. However, Lynch also noted that faculty members need to be deep experts in a core discipline (e.g., civil engineering) and that their preparation should reflect a balance between theory and applied research. Lynch further noted that applications for faculty positions concentrated on CPS may not have been strong because the candidates do not have the expected depth in more traditional areas. Similarly, junior faculty may find themselves in departments where the senior faculty have dissimilar backgrounds and research and teaching interests.

Several speakers stressed the value of hands-on projects. Philip Koopman, Carnegie Mellon University, noted that the tools needed to provide students with this experience must incorporate the challenges of large-scale systems and are often expensive and require frequent technology refreshes. Koopman also explained that developing problems that represent the complexity of CPS is difficult. Projects and problems must be realistic and motivating but also incorporate domain knowledge that is accessible to students. There is a risk that problems can become overly complicated—projects must be designed with the right amount of "messy."

MAKING CPS MORE ATTRACTIVE TO STUDENTS

In addition to recruiting faculty, universities will need to ensure that CPS is attractive to students. Several presenters reported that students tend to be attracted to courses that emphasize robotics or the Internet of things but hesitate to register for courses that specifically reference CPS.

Additionally, presenters from both industry and academia observed that large information technology (IT) firms like Facebook and Google have captured the imagination of undergraduates in a way that many CPS-intensive firms have not, even though CPS work also provides significant opportunities to innovate and have considerable real-world impact. Several asked how these opportunities can best be communicated to current and prospective students.

CPS EDUCATION OPPORTUNITIES BEYOND THE UNDERGRADUATE CLASSROOM

Although the workshop presentations and JPL briefing were largely focused on 4-year undergraduate programs and subsequent graduate programs (to some degree), some talks also touched on opportunities to introduce CPS concepts in K-12 education and supplement CPS education and training through industry-academic partnerships, internships, and online, post-graduate continuing education.

Industry-Academic Partnerships

Dimitri Mavris discussed efforts in his laboratory, the Georgia Institute of Technology's Aerospace Systems Design Laboratory (ASDL), to bridge the gap between the kinds of CPS-related research that students are typically exposed to in academia and the kinds of research carried out in industry. In the ASDL program, students are engaged for two semesters in open-ended, interdisciplinary, and large-scale projects. The problems require practical implementation of advanced methods that go beyond those needed in typical senior design problems. In one case, General Electric provided ASDL with a set of problems whose solution would require student teams with strong foundations in power technology, software, and complex system design and analysis. Five interdisciplinary teams were created with students from electrical engineering, systems engineering (from the aerospace engineering department), and management programs. An industry representative who provided practical advice and technical feedback, and course correction as needed, advised the students.

Mavris described several challenges faced by students grappling with the inherently interdisciplinary nature of the problems. For example, systems engineering students felt they lacked sufficient expertise in electrical engineering while at the same time the EE students did not always accept the architectural work being done by the systems engineers. Over time, the students' knowledge and appreciation of the contributions that each discipline could make to the team effort grew, as did trust and the quality of the collaboration.

Also, the teams found they had gaps in their collective knowledge in such areas as practical consideration of real power flow systems, systems engineering fundamentals, economic and market opportunity analysis, and impact of grid regulation on solution viability. Students also struggled with the business aspects of the project—overexplaining the structure and value of smart grid systems solutions and struggling with business plan development for products or services. Students also tended to rush into design activities before fully exploring alternatives.

Mavris cited several ingredients for a successful research partnership program. Both faculty and the industry partner must be very committed, and the students must be highly motivated, competitive, inventive, and articulate. Success is most likely when the industry problems are aligned with faculty expertise and research activities. The intellectual property issues inherent in working with industry will also require attention and appropriate coordination mechanisms.

Internships

Steve Anton, Tennessee Technological University, described his experience with Los Alamos National Laboratory's Dynamics Summer School. The 9-week intensive summer program assigns a staff mentor to students and allows students to learn more about CPS and carry out research. Anton observed that some students enter the school relatively unfamiliar with CPS, and many are unfamiliar with key topics such as sensing, data acquisition, and signal processing. The students participate in week-long tutorials on sensors, controls, signal processing, and embedded systems. Students also participate in laboratory research, gaining familiarity with research practices and laboratory equipment, and develop teamwork and technical writing skills. Because it is designed to be multidisciplinary, the program works well to break down boundaries among mechanical, electrical, and computer engineers and scientists. An additional benefit to students' future careers in CPS is that they develop contacts in the CPS technical community.

Massive Open Online Courses

Magnus Egerstedt, Georgia Institute of Technology, described his experiences developing and teaching a CPS-related massive open online course (MOOC). Egerstedt had taught an embedded and hybrid control systems course at the senior undergraduate level to students from electrical, computer, mechanical, and aerospace engineering and computer science and sought to provide a more solid grounding in theory as well as additional opportunities to apply that theory in practice. A stronger theoretical foundation would allow students who otherwise tended to approach difficult problems by patching the code to use more formal and systematic approaches. "Flipping the classroom" by using a MOOC to cover the theory component would maximize the classroom time available to apply the theory to robotics laboratories.

Topics for the MOOC included an introduction to controls, mobile robots, linear systems, control design, hybrid systems, navigation problems, and, finally, connecting these elements. Initial enrollment in the 2013 course was around 40,000; about 7,000 remained active at the end of the session.[2] Students passing 65 percent of quizzes received a certificate of completion, and those passing 90 percent received a certificate of distinction. Egerstedt was also surprised that several of those enrolled were practicing engineers who wanted to revisit the topic.

On the practice side, Egerstedt was unhappy with the available choices for educational robots, so his team developed its own, the Quick-Bot. This robot has a differential drive, four infrared inputs, WiFi, and optical encoders and uses BeagleBone Black and Arduino computers. The cost is approximately $150 to $300. Egerstedt worked with hardware companies and online electronics providers to ensure that parts were available. Lessons were provided to help students build their own robots.

Egerstedt noted several challenges. The project was incredibly difficult, requiring three times the work of a regular class. Dividing what would normally be 90-minute lectures into very short sublectures typical of MOOCs is hard, and writing multiple-choice questions on a complex topic like control theory is incredibly difficult. Egerstedt also noted that

---

[2] Edward Lee, University of California, Berkeley, also spoke briefly of teaching a CPS MOOC based on his embedded systems course. Offered during the summer of 2014, the course provided virtual laboratory software. The course was 6 weeks long and included 49 lectures (approximately 11 hours of video) and 6 weekly laboratory assignments. Peak enrollment was 8,767, with 2,213 submitting at least one assignment. Approximately 1,543 scored above a 0, and only 342 "passed."

the overall design for a CPS course is challenging. For example, what are the prerequisites, what are appropriate assignments and laboratories, and how multidisciplinary should the lessons be?

Egerstedt concluded by expressing excitement about CPS as a new field and the pedagogical potential of flipped classrooms using MOOCs. There is a serious appetite for CPS content, and Egerstedt found that other schools were using his MOOC to flip their own classrooms. Egerstedt also suggested that MOOCs could be used to help students lacking prerequisite material or to supplement faculty capabilities.

K-12 Education

Harry Cheng discussed his work in incorporating CPS into K-12 education at the University of California, Davis, Center for Integrated Computing and Science, Technology, Engineering, and Mathematics (C-STEM). C-STEM was created to close the achievement gap by broadening participation of traditionally underrepresented students in computing and STEM-related careers. C-STEM incorporates computing and robotics, two areas that touch on CPS core knowledge, into the K-12 curriculum by finding ways to use them to teach mathematics and other core subjects. The C-STEM curriculum, outlined in Figure 1.4, is accepted as part of the subject matter admission requirements of the University of California

Elementary School Curriculum
- Exploring Math with Robotics and Computing

Middle School Curriculum
- Math 7 with Computing
- Math 8 with Computing
- Computer Programming with Ch (a C/C++ interpreter)
- Robotics and Video Production

High School Curriculum
- Algebra 1 with Computing (math)
- Algebra 1 with Computing and Robotics (math)
- Integrated Math 1 with Computing (math)
- Integrated Math 1 with Computing and Robotics (math)
- Introduction to Computer Programming with C (elective)
- Computing with Robotics (elective)
- Introduction to Computer Programming for Engineering Applications (a University of California, Davis, engineering course)
- Computer Science Principles (elective)
- Principles and Design of Cyber-Physical Systems (elective)

FIGURE 1.4 C-STEM Curriculum. SOURCE: Harry H. Cheng, UC Davis Center for Integrated Computing and STEM Education (C-STEM), University of California, Davis.

system, allowing California schools to adopt the curriculum. In addition to developing the curriculum, C-STEM supports K-12 teacher development via a summer institute, academic year workshops, onsite training, and periodic conferences. Furthermore, C-STEM supports numerous robotic competitions that develop student skills and foster interest in the curriculum.

2

Preliminary Observations

The committee has developed a preliminary set of observations about cyber-physical systems (CPS) education based on the presentations and briefing summarized in Chapter 1 as well as from its own expertise and deliberations thus far. The committee will continue its information gathering and deliberations and will issue its final report providing its findings and recommendations later in 2015.

- *CPS skills and experience are in demand.* The anecdotal reports from industry representatives point to two areas of demand. First, as CPS becomes an increasingly important aspect of products and services, some companies are looking specifically for people with an educational concentration in CPS—who some dubbed the "CPS engineer." Second, CPS skills are becoming increasingly important across a wide range of engineering specialties. Although it is difficult to quantify the demand, more than one presenter observed that his firm was hampered in developing new products because it was not able to secure sufficient CPS talent. Others noted difficulties in hiring people with the CPS skills they were looking for; one response has been for some organizations to focus on using on-the-job training to develop additional CPS skills internally.
- *A lack of familiarity with the term "cyber-physical systems" itself may impede student interest in the field.* Although cyber-physical systems have been widely used and designed for some time now, perspective students may not perceive CPS as an attractive area of study and work in part because they do not recognize the label. By contrast, students are often

eager to enroll in courses with "robotics" or the Internet of things in their title. Both of these overlap with CPS, although they may not cover all of the foundations needed for CPS. Also, large information technology firms like Facebook and Google have captured the imagination of students in a way that many CPS-intensive firms have not, even though the latter provide significant opportunities to innovate and have considerable real-world impact.

- *"CPS engineering"[1] may be emerging as a distinct field of engineering.* CPS draws knowledge and approaches from multiple areas of engineering and may indeed have significant overlap with other areas of engineering; however, CPS has begun to take on a distinctive character.

Given that CPS is multidisciplinary and draws from many areas, it indeed has significant overlap with those areas. However, CPS is distinctive due to several qualities. For example, embedded systems often concentrate on low-cost, simple devices or large and complex systems embedded in closed or very controlled environments. Today, most new embedded systems are in environments that are open via connections (giving us the "cyber" in CPS) to the wireless world and the Internet. Systems engineering also contributes heavily to CPS. However, systems engineering typically concentrates on the organization, management, and integration required for large systems but does not deeply address the detailed technological needs that arise in combining the physical with the cyber. Several examples of CPS, such as autonomous vehicles, could be considered "robotics." However, classical robots do not necessarily draw on the CPS principles needed for autonomous vehicles: real-time, safety-critical, large-scale, wireless communication environments and operation in unconstrained environments.

- *There is growing agreement on the core elements of CPS, but a diverse set of approaches to fashioning CPS programs is likely and appropriate.* It seems possible to outline a set of core concepts, principles, and themes, and the committee will be endeavoring to use this to lay out a model undergraduate curriculum in CPS for its final report. That said, CPS is new and its applications are continuing to emerge and evolve, suggesting that an even higher degree of variation among approaches will be found than already exists across engineering and computer science programs at different institutions. Multiple pathways toward CPS-focused programs are also likely. Programs have already grown organically from computer science and electrical engineering programs; these programs will continue to

---

[1] The committee uses the terms "CPS engineering" and "CPS engineer" to mean a set of skills and knowledge needed to design and build a CPS, and a person with those skills; the terms are not limited to a set of credentials or to someone who has a degree or certification in CPS.

grow organically and follow somewhat distinct trajectories. At the same time, engineering programs in areas such as such civil, mechanical, and aerospace have been placing increasing emphasis on CPS—a trend that seems likely to continue and spread.

- *The need for CPS skills is becoming pervasive across engineering and computer science.* CPS are deployed in a variety of domains, including civil, mechanical, and aerospace. CPS engineers will not replace the need for engineering that focuses on deep understanding of topics specific to these fields, but people with such skills will increasingly be central to engineering teams. The other engineers and computer scientists on those teams will increasingly need at least some CPS knowledge and skills.
- *It will likely not be sufficient to simply bundle existing courses to create a CPS program.* Although many of the topics in CPS can also be found in current engineering and computer science courses, the emphasis on the interaction of the cyber and the physical is unique to CPS. For example, control theory classes in electrical engineering typically focus on electromagnetic principles such as those for circuits. A CPS control theory course would need to better incorporate topics related to networks, human-in-the-loop models, security, software, and real-time and hybrid control. Similarly, a computer science department's software design course tends to employ non-physical world applications; a CPS course would need to emphasize physical constraints.
- *CPS education programs need to include a hands-on component.* These opportunities can be provided to students via an interdisciplinary capstone course, extensive course-specific laboratories, an engineering elective course focused on a single project, or internships and industry-academic partnerships.
- *Other paths to CPS knowledge will be important.* Although this study will focus on 4-year undergraduate curricula, other paths for students and the workforce to gain CPS knowledge are also important. These paths include minors or certificates and graduate programs within other disciplines, opportunities for community and vocational schools and post-graduate professional studies, the use of online education or massive open online courses, and the role of K-12 education in preparing students for a range of careers involving CPS.

The committee also identified several challenges in creating and supporting cyber-physical systems programs at universities. The committee will explore possible solutions in its final report.

- *Working across disciplinary and department boundaries can create significant challenges.* CPS exists at the intersection of multiple disciplines. This has significant impact on how a curriculum will be developed and taught. Organically developed CPS activities have generally grown out of electrical engineering or computer science departments; however, to develop the best students, a degree program would need to incorporate both of these departments, plus inclusion of domain-specific departments such as aerospace or civil engineering.

- *A significant challenge will be identifying, recruiting, and educating appropriate faculty members to teach new and different courses.* Many universities currently have a limited handful of faculty who can teach CPS courses. If schools are to develop and offer a full CPS curriculum, additional faculty members will be needed. Additionally, the interdisciplinary nature of CPS can create challenges for faculty in securing research funding and obtaining tenure. Alternative paths, such as hiring non-tenure-track professors from industry, may need to be explored.

- *Textbooks, curricular materials, and laboratory facilities will need to be developed.* Developing these critical resources requires both time and financial support.

Appendixes

A

Biographies of Committee Members and Staff

JOHN A. (JACK) STANKOVIC, *Co-Chair*, is currently the BP America Professor in the Computer Science Department at the University of Virginia (UVA). He came to UVA as BP America Professor and chair of the Department of Computer Science in 1997. Professor Stankovic is a fellow of the Institute of Electrical and Electronics Engineers (IEEE) and the Association for Computing Machinery (ACM), and he served on the Computing Research Association board of directors for 9 years. He currently serves on the National Research Council's (NRC's) Computer Science Telecommunications Board (CSTB). He received the IEEE Award for Outstanding Technical Contributions and Leadership in Real-Time Systems. He also received the IEEE TC on Distributed Processing Annual Distinguished Achievement Award in 2006 as the inaugural winner. Professor Stankovic received an Outstanding Scholar Award from the University of Massachusetts. He also received a Distinguished Faculty Award from the School of Engineering at UVA. He was co-founder and co-editor-in-chief of the *International Journal on Real-Time Systems*, editor-in-chief of *IEEE Transactions on Parallel and Distributed Computing*, associate editor for *ACM Transactions on Wireless Sensor Networks*, associate editor for *ACM Transactions on Embedded Systems*, and book series editor for *Real-Time Systems*. He has won 11 best paper awards and has an h-index of 103. Dr. Stankovic received his Ph.D. from Brown University and then served on the faculty of the University of Massachusetts, Amherst.

JAMES (JIM) STURGES, *Co-Chair*, is an independent consultant specializing in program management and systems engineering for very large, complex aerospace and defense systems. He retired in 2009 from Lockheed Martin Corporation, where he had been director, engineering processes, and director, mission assurance. Prior to that he was vice president, engineering and total quality, at Loral Air Traffic Control/Lockheed Martin Air Traffic Management, and C3I Strategic Business area director for Loral Tactical Defense Systems in Arizona. He is an associate fellow and past member of the Standards Executive Council and chair of the Systems Engineering Technical Committee of the American Institute of Aeronautics and Astronautics (AIAA) and was twice chair of the corporate advisory board for the International Council on Systems Engineering. Early in his career, he was a naval aviator, instrument instructor, and check pilot and anti-submarine warfare officer for the U.S. Navy. He has a B.A. from the University of North Carolina and an M.S. and aeronautical engineering degree from the Naval Postgraduate School at Monterey.

ALEXANDRE BAYEN is currently an associate chancellor professor at the University of California, Berkeley. He has been the director of the Institute for Transportation Studies (ITS) since 2014. He was a visiting researcher at NASA Ames Research Center from 2000 to 2003. Between January 2004 and December 2004, he worked as the research director of the Autonomous Navigation Laboratory at the Laboratoire de Recherches Balistiques et Aerodynamiques (Ministere de la Defense, Vernon, France), where he holds the rank of major. Dr. Bayen has authored two books and more than 150 articles in peer-reviewed journals and conferences. He is the recipient of the Ballhaus Award from Stanford University (2004) and the CAREER award from the National Science Foundation (2009), and he is a NASA Top 10 Innovator on Water Sustainability (2010). His projects Mobile Century and Mobile Millennium received the 2008 Best of ITS Award for Best Innovative Practice at the ITS World Congress and a TRANNY Award from the California Transportation Foundation (2009). Mobile Millennium has been featured more than 200 times in the media, including TV and radio (CBS, NBC, ABC, CNET, NPR, KGO, the BBC) as well as in the popular press (*Wall Street Journal*, *Washington Post*, *LA Times*). Dr. Bayen is the recipient of the Presidential Early Career Award for Scientists and Engineers (PECASE) from the White House (2010) and the recipient of the Okawa Research Grant Award, the Ruberti Prize from IEEE, and the Huber Prize from ASCE. He received an engineering degree in applied mathematics from the Ecole Polytechnique, France; an M.S. degree in aeronautics and astronautics from Stanford University, and a Ph.D. in aeronautics and astronautics from Stanford University.

CHARLES R. FARRAR is an adjunct professor in the Structural Engineering Department at the University of California, San Diego (UCSD). From 1989 to 1996, he served as an adjunct professor at the University of New Mexico's Department of Mechanical/Civil Engineering. He also serves as the Engineering Institute Leader at Los Alamos National Laboratory (LANL) and is the 2010 Distinguished Bromilow Lecturer. He is currently working jointly with the engineering faculty at UCSD to develop the Los Alamos/UCSD Engineering Institute, with a research focus on multidisciplinary projects that integrate advanced predictive modeling, novel sensing systems, and new approaches to information technology. He has 27 years' experience at LANL. Dr. Farrar's research interests focus on developing integrated hardware and software solutions to structural health monitoring problems. The results of this research have been documented in more than 300 publications as well as numerous keynote lectures at international conferences. Additional professional activities include current appointments to associate editor positions for the *International Journal of Structural Health Monitoring* and *Earthquake Engineering and Structural Dynamics* and the development of a short course entitled "Structural Health Monitoring: A Statistical Pattern Recognition Approach," which has been offered more than 17 times to industry and government agencies in Asia, Australia, Europe, and the United States. In 2007 he was elected a fellow of the American Society of Mechanical Engineers. Dr. Farrar received a Ph.D. in civil engineering from the University of New Mexico.

MARYE ANNE FOX is the former chancellor of UCSD. Dr. Fox is a member of the National Academy of Sciences and has received honorary degrees from 12 institutions in the United States and abroad. In October 2010, President Barack Obama awarded her the National Medal of Science, the highest honor bestowed by the U.S. government on scientists, engineers, and inventors. Previously, Dr. Fox was chancellor at North Carolina State University, and she spent 22 years at the University of Texas, where she advanced to vice president for research and held the Waggoner Regents Chair in chemistry. She earned a bachelor's degree in science from Notre Dame College, a master's degree in science from Cleveland State University, and a Ph.D. in chemistry from Dartmouth College.

SANTIAGO GRIJALVA is an associate professor of electrical and computer engineering at the Georgia Institute of Technology. He joined the faculty in 2009. He is the director of the Advanced Computational Electricity Systems (ACES) Laboratory, where he conducts research on real-time power system control, informatics, and economics and renewable energy integration in power. In spring 2012, Dr. Grijalva was appointed as the Strategic Energy Institute (SEI) associate director for electricity systems, responsible for coordinating large efforts on electricity research and policy at Georgia Tech. He was a postdoctoral fellow in Power and Energy Systems at the University of Illinois from 2003 to 2004. From 1995 to 1997, he was with the Ecuadorian National Center for Energy Control as engineer and manager of the Real-Time EMS Software Department. From 2002 to 2009, he was with PowerWorld Corporation as a senior software architect and developer of innovative real-time and optimization applications used today by utilities, control centers, and universities in more than 60 countries. Dr. Grijalva is a leading researcher on ultra-reliable architectures for critical energy infrastructures. He has pioneered work on decentralized and autonomous power system control, renewable energy integration in power, and unified network models and applications. He is currently the principal investigator (PI) of various future electricity grid research projects for the Department of Energy, the Advanced Research Projects Agency—Energy, the Electric Power Research Institute, and the Power Systems Engineering Research Center as well as other government organizations, research consortia, and industrial sponsors. Dr. Grijalva received an electrical engineer degree from EPN-Ecuador in 1994, an M.S. certificate in information systems from ESPE-Ecuador, and M.S. and Ph.D. degrees in electrical engineering from the University of Illinois, Urbana-Champaign.

HIMANSHU KHURANA is the senior manager for the Integrated Security Technologies section of the Knowledge Systems Laboratory at Honeywell Automation and Control Systems. The Integrated Security Technologies section focuses on research, development, and technology transition in cybersecurity, computer vision, surveillance, and biometrics. Dr. Khurana's research interests lie in the area of distributed system security, especially as applied to large-scale distributed systems and critical infrastructures, and he has published 50 articles in this area. Prior to joining Honeywell, he was with the University of Illinois, Urbana-Champaign, and served as the co-PI for the Trustworthy Cyber Infrastructure for Power Center (now the TCIPG). He has been involved with several Smart Grid initiatives, including the North American Synchrophasor Initiative; the NIST Cyber Security Working Group; and the DNP3 Technical Committee, as well as in developing relevant cybersecurity standards. He obtained his M.S. and Ph.D. degrees from the University of Maryland, College Park.

PANGANAMALA R. (PR) KUMAR is a professor of computer science at Texas A&M University, where he holds the College of Engineering Chair in Computer Engineering. From 1977 to 1984 he was a faculty member in the Department of Mathematics at the University of Maryland, Baltimore County, and from 1985 to 2011 he was a faculty member in the Department of Electrical and Computer Engineering and the Coordinated Science Laboratory at the University of Illinois. Dr. Kumar has worked on problems in game theory, adaptive control, stochastic systems, simulated annealing, neural networks, machine learning, queuing networks, manufacturing systems, scheduling, wafer fabrication plants, and information theory. His current research interests are in wireless networks, sensor networks, and networked embedded control systems. His research is currently focused on wireless networks; sensor networks; cyber-physical systems; and the convergence of control, communication, and computation. Dr. Kumar is a member of the National Academy of Engineering and the Academy of Sciences of the Developing World. He was awarded an honorary doctorate by the Swiss Federal Institute of Technology (Eidgenossische Technische Hochschule) in Zurich. He received the IEEE Field Award for Control Systems, the Donald P. Eckman Award of the American Automatic Control Council, the Fred W. Ellersick Prize of the IEEE Communications Society, and the Outstanding Contribution Award of ACM SIGMOBILE. He is a fellow of IEEE. He was a guest chair professor and leader of the Guest Chair Professor Group on Wireless Communication and Networking at Tsinghua University, Beijing, China. He is a D.J. Gandhi Distinguished Visiting Professor at IIT Bombay. He is an honorary professor at IIT Hyderabad. He was awarded the Distinguished Alumnus Award from IIT Madras, the Alumni Achievement Award from Washington University in St. Louis, and the Daniel C. Drucker Eminent Faculty Award from the College of Engineering at the University of Illinois. Dr. Kumar obtained his B. Tech. degree in electrical engineering (electronics) from I.I.T. Madras and his M.S. and D.Sc. degrees in systems science and mathematics from Washington University in St. Louis.

INSUP LEE is the Cecilia Fitler Moore Professor of Computer and Information Science and director of Penn Research in Embedded Computing and Integrated Systems Engineering (PRECISE) Center, which he founded in 2008, at the University of Pennsylvania. He also holds a secondary appointment in the Department of Electrical and Systems Engineering. His research interests include cyber-physical systems (CPS), real-time systems, embedded and hybrid systems, formal methods and tools, high-confidence medical device systems, run-time verification, software certification, and trust management. The theme of his research activities has been to assure and improve the correctness, safety, and timeliness of life-critical embedded systems. Dr. Lee and his student received the best paper award at IEEE Real-Time Systems Symposium (RTSS) 2003 for their work on compositional schedulability analysis. His papers also received the best paper award at IEEE RTSS 2012, the best student paper at IEEE Real-Time and Embedded Technology and Applications Symposium (RTAS) 2012, and the co-best paper at the Council of European Aerospace Societies in 2011. Recently, he has been working in medical CPS and security of CPS. He has served on many program committees and chaired several international conferences and workshops and has also served on various steering and advisory committees of technical societies. He has served on the editorial boards of several scientific journals, including *IEEE Transactions on Computers*, *Formal Methods in System Design*, and *Real-Time Systems Journal*. He is a founding co-editor-in-chief of *KIISE Journal of Computing Science and Engineering*. He was a chair of the IEEE Computer Society Technical Committee on Real-Time Systems and an IEEE CS Distinguished Visitor Speaker. He was a member of the Technical Advisory Group of the President's Council of Advisors on Science and Technology Networking and Information Technology. He received an appreciation plaque from the Ministry of Science, IT and Future Planning, South Korea, for speaking at the ULTRA Program Forum in 2013. He is an IEEE fellow and received the IEEE TC-RTS Outstanding Technical Achievement and Leadership Award in 2008. He received a B.S. degree with honors in mathematics from the University of North Carolina, Chapel Hill, and a Ph.D. degree in computer science from the University of Wisconsin, Madison.

WILLIAM MILAM is a technical expert at the Ford Research and Innovation Center, Ford Motor Company. His research addresses modeling and implementation of advanced technology automotive engines for improved fuel economy and emissions, and improvements in systems engineering processes for the design of automotive embedded systems. He is a senior member of IEEE and a member of the Society of Automotive Engineers (SAE). Mr. Milam serves as a member of the SAE Electronic Design Automation Standards Committee and the SAE Architecture Analysis and Design Language Standards Committee and chairs the SAE Model Based Embedded Systems Engineering Task Force.

SANJOY K. MITTER joined the Massachusetts Institute of Technology (MIT) in 1969, where he has been a professor of electrical engineering since 1973. His current research interests are communication and control in a networked environment, the relationship of statistical and quantum physics to information theory and control and autonomy and adaptiveness for integrative organization. He taught at Case Western Reserve University from 1965 to 1969. He was the director of the MIT Laboratory for Information and Decision Systems from 1981 to 1999. He has also been a professor of mathematics at the Scuola Normale, Pisa, Italy, from 1986 to

1996. He has held visiting positions at Imperial College, London; University of Groningen, Holland; INRIA, France; Tata Institute of Fundamental Research, India; ETH, Zurich, Switzerland; and several American universities. Professor Mitter was an Ulam Scholar at Los Alamos National Laboratory and a John von Neumann Visiting Professor in Mathematics at the Technical University of Munich, Germany. He was awarded the AACC Richard E. Bellman Control Heritage Award for 2007. He was the McKay Professor at the University of California, Berkeley, in March 2000, and held the Russell-Severance-Springer Chair in fall 2003. He is a fellow of IEEE and a member of the National Academy of Engineering. He is the winner of the 2000 IEEE Control Systems award. He was elected a foreign member of Instituto Veneto di Scienze, ed Arti in 2003. Professor Mitter received his Ph.D. degree from the Imperial College of Science and Technology.

JOSÉ M.F. MOURA is Philip and Marsha Dowd University Professor of Electrical and Computer Engineering at Carnegie Mellon University (CMU) and, by courtesy, a professor of biomedical engineering. He is a member of the National Academy of Engineers, a corresponding member of the Portugal Academy of Science, an IEEE fellow, and a fellow of the American Association for the Advancement of Science (AAAS). He has been a visiting professor at New York University and MIT and a visiting scholar at the University of Southern California, and was on the faculty of IST (Portugal). Dr. Moura's research interests are in data science and statistical signal and image processing. Current research projects include data analytics for unstructured big data, distributed inference in networks, SPIRAL (an intelligent compiler), nondestructive health monitoring systems, bioimaging, signal processing on graphs, and image/video processing. Dr. Moura received the IEEE Signal Processing Society Award for outstanding technical contributions and leadership in signal processing and the IEEE Signal Processing Society Technical Achievement Award for fundamental contributions to statistical signal processing. He is on the board of directors of IEEE and served as IEEE Division IX Director. He was the president of the IEEE Signal Processing Society. He was editor-in-chief of *IEEE Transactions on Signal Processing* and acting editor-in-chief for *IEEE Signal Processing Letters*. He was on the editorial board of several journals, including *ACM Transactions on Sensor Networks* and *IEEE Proceedings*. He was on the steering committees of the IEEE International Symposium on Bioimaging and the ACM/IEEE International Symposium on Information Processing in Sensor Networks. He serves or served on several IEEE boards and chaired the Technical Activities Board Transactions Committee. He holds a D.Sc. in electrical engineering and computer science, an M.Sc., and EE degrees, all from MIT, and an EE degree from Instituto Superior Técnico (IST, Portugal).

GEORGE J. PAPPAS is the Joseph Moore Professor and chair of the Department of Electrical and Systems Engineering at the University of Pennsylvania. He also holds a secondary appointment in the Departments of Computer and Information Sciences, and Mechanical Engineering and Applied Mechanics. He is a member of the General Robotics Automation Sensing and Perception Laboratory and the PRECISE Center. He has previously served as the deputy dean for research in the School of Engineering and Applied Science. His research focuses on control theory and, in particular, hybrid systems, embedded systems, and hierarchical and distributed control systems, with applications to unmanned aerial vehicles, distributed robotics, green buildings, and biomolecular networks. He is a fellow of IEEE and has received various awards, such as the Antonio Ruberti Young Researcher Prize, the George S. Axelby Award, and the National Science Foundation Presidential Early Career Award for Scientists and Engineers.

PAULO TABUADA is a professor of electrical engineering and vice chair for graduate affairs at the University of California, Los Angeles (UCLA). Between January 2002 and July 2003, he was a postdoctoral researcher at the University of Pennsylvania. After spending 3 years at the University of Notre Dame as an assistant professor, he joined the Electrical Engineering Department at UCLA, where he established and directs the Cyber-Physical Systems Laboratory. His research interests include modeling, analysis, design, control, and security of CPS. He received his Licenciatura degree in aerospace engineering from the Instituto Superior Técnico, Lisbon, Portugal, and his Ph.D. degree in electrical and computer engineering from the Institute for Systems and Robotics, a private research institute associated with Instituto Superior Tecnico. Dr. Tabuada's contributions to CPS have been recognized by multiple awards, including the NSF CAREER award in 2005, the Donald P. Eckman award in 2009, and the George S. Axelby award in 2011. In 2009, he co-chaired the International Conference Hybrid Systems: Computation and Control, and in 2012 he was program co-chair for the Third International Federation for Automatic Control Workshop on Distributed Estimation and Control in Networked Systems. He also served on the editorial board of *IEEE Embedded Systems Letters* and *IEEE Transactions on Automatic Control*. His latest book, on verification and control of hybrid systems, was published in 2009.

MANUELA M. VELOSO is Herbert A. Simon Professor in the Computer Science Department, School of Computer Science, at Carnegie Mellon

University (CMU). She holds courtesy appointments in the Robotics Institute, Machine Learning, Electrical and Computer Engineering, and Mechanical Engineering Departments. Dr. Veloso conducts research in artificial intelligence and robotics. She founded and directs the CORAL research laboratory at CMU for the study of multiagent systems where agents "collaborate, observe, reason, act, and learn." She is an IEEE fellow, AAAS fellow, and Association for the Advancement of Artificial Intelligence (AAAI) fellow. She is the current president of AAAI and past president of the RoboCup Federation. She received the 2009 ACM/SIGART Autonomous Agents Research Award for her contributions to agents in uncertain and dynamic environments, including distributed robot localization and world modeling, strategy selection in multiagent systems in the presence of adversaries, and robot learning from demonstration. Dr. Veloso and her students have contributed a variety of autonomous robots for robot soccer, education, and service. More recently, she introduced symbiotic robot autonomy, in which robots are autonomous but aware of their perceptual, cognitive, and actuation limitations and can proactively ask for help from humans, other robots, and the web. For the past 3 years, following robust localization, task planning, and symbiotic autonomy, her collaborative service robots, CoBots, have navigated for more than 200 km in the multi-floor buildings at CMU. Dr. Veloso holds a Ph.D. in computer science from CMU and B.Sc. and M.Sc. degrees in electrical and computer engineering from the Instituto Superior Tecnico, Lisbon, Portugal.

Staff

JON EISENBERG is director of the CSTB. He has also been study director for a diverse body of work, including a series of studies exploring Internet and broadband policy and networking and communications technologies. In 1995-1997 he was a AAAS Science, Engineering, and Diplomacy Fellow at the U.S. Agency for International Development, where he worked on technology transfer and information and telecommunications policy issues. Dr. Eisenberg received his Ph.D. in physics from the University of Washington and a B.S. in physics with honors from the University of Massachusetts, Amherst.

VIRGINIA BACON TALATI is a program officer for the CSTB. She formerly served as a program associate with the Frontiers of Engineering program at the National Academy of Engineering. Prior to her work at the Academies, she served as a senior project assistant in Education Technology at the National School Boards Association. Ms. Bacon Talati has a B.S. in science, technology, and culture from the Georgia Institute of Technology and an M.P.P. from George Mason University, with a focus on science and technology policy.

SHENAE BRADLEY is a senior program assistant at the CSTB. She currently provides support for the Committee on Sustaining Growth in Computing Performance, the Committee on Wireless Technology Prospects and Policy Options, and the Computational Thinking for Everyone: A Workshop Series Planning Committee, to name a few. Prior to this, she served as an administrative assistant for the Ironworker Management Progressive Action Cooperative Trust and managed a number of apartment rental communities for Edgewood Management Corporation in the Maryland/D.C./Delaware metropolitan areas.

B

Presentations to the Committee

This interim report refers to presentations to the committee at two workshops and one briefing.

- Workshop on 21st Century Cyber-Physical Systems Education: Defining Needs and Identifying Challenges, April 30, 2014, Washington, D.C.
    — Dick Bulterman, FX Palo Alto Laboratory (FXPAL)
    — David Corman, National Science Foundation
    — Ryan Izard, Clemson University
    — Dan Johnson, Honeywell International, Inc.
    — Kevin Massey, Defense Advanced Research Projects Agency
    — John Mills, SimuQuest, Inc.
    — Sanjai Rayadurgam, University of Minnesota
    — Alberto Sangiovanna-Vincentelli, University of California, Berkeley
    — Lucio Soibelman, University of Southern California
    — Craig Stephens, Ford Research and Advanced Engineering, Ford Motor Company
    — Joe Salvo, GE Research
    — Janos Sztipanovits, Vanderbilt University
    — Jon Williams, John Deere

- Workshop on 21st Century Cyber-Physical Systems Education: Developing Solutions, October 2-3, 2014, Washington, D.C.
    — Tarek Abdelzaher, University of Illinois, Urbana-Champaign
    — Douglas Adams, Vanderbilt University
    — Steve Anton, Tennessee Technological University
    — Harry Cheng, University of California, Davis
    — André DeHon, University of Pennsylvania
    — Magnus Egerstedt, Georgia Institute of Technology
    — Norman Fortenberry, American Society for Engineering Education
    — Christopher Gill, Washington University in St. Louis
    — Scott Hareland, Medtronic, Inc.
    — Jonathan How, Massachusetts Institute of Technology
    — Clas Jacobson, United Technologies Corporation
    — Philip Koopman, Carnegie Mellon University
    — Edward Lee, University of California, Berkeley
    — Jerry Lynch, University of Michigan
    — Dimitri Mavris, Georgia Institute of Technology
    — Shankar Sastry, University of California, Berkeley
    — Henning Schulzrinne, Columbia University

- Briefing to the committee by Daniel Dvorak and David Nichols, Jet Propulsion Laboratory, June 26, 2014, via teleconference